THE FACTS ON
ANGELS

D1462174

John Ankerberg
& John Weldon

HARVEST HOUSE PUBLISHERS
Eugene, Oregon 97402

Other books by
John Ankerberg and John Weldon

The Facts on Angels

The Facts on Astrology

The Facts on Creation vs. Evolution

The Facts on the Faith Movement

*The Facts on False Teaching
in the Church*

The Facts on Halloween

*The Facts on Holistic Health
and the New Medicine*

The Facts on Homosexuality

The Facts on Islam

The Facts on the Jehovah's Witnesses

The Facts on the King James Only Debate

The Facts on the Masonic Lodge

The Facts on the Mormon Church

The Facts on the New Age Movement

The Facts on the Occult

The Facts on Psychic Readings

The Facts on Rock Music

The Facts on Roman Catholicism

*The Facts on UFOs
and Other Supernatural Phenomena*

FACTS ON ANGELS

Copyright © 1995 by The Ankerberg Theological Research Institute
Published by Harvest House Publishers
Eugene, Oregon 97042

ISBN 1-56507-345-2

Contents

Preface: Angels, Angels, Everywhere

Introduction

Section I
The Good Angels

Section II
Modern Angel Encounters:
The Popular Angels

PREFACE
Angels, Angels, Everywhere

Why is it important that we know about angels? Angels constitute one of the most intriguing subjects one could ever study. Leading philosopher Mortimer J. Adler, editor of the *Encyclopedia Britannica* and architect of *The Great Books of the Western World* series, recently stated that angels were more fascinating than either science fiction or the concept of extraterrestrial beings.[1] Why is this?

According to the Bible, angels have literally shaped the course of human history and continue to do so today. Consider the fallen angel in the Garden who slyly engineered the moral fall of the entire human race (Genesis 3). Or the angels who spoke and mediated the law of Moses, which literally changed the Western world (Acts 7:53; Hebrews 2:2). Or the literally thousands of "angelic" encounters throughout history in the lives of ordinary and famous individuals including Abraham Lincoln, boxer Evander Holyfield, and rock stars George Harrison and Carlos Santana (who invokes the presence of angels before each concert).[2] The noted mystic William Blake said he was under the guidance of "angels" night and day.[3]

From the the terrifying angels of the book of Revelation—whose power over nature and humanity is so awesome simple mortals can hardly comprehend it (Revelation 8:6-12; 9:15)—to the angels who helped Christ in His wilderness and Gethsemane temptations and assisted the early church (Matthew 4:6,11; Luke 22:43; Acts 10:22; 12:7) angels have influenced, either directly or indirectly, the lives of everyone on earth.

The world is, quite literally, alive with angels. In its cover story on angels, *Time* magazine for December 27, 1993, observed, "If there is such a thing as a universal idea, common across cultures and through the centuries, the belief in angels comes close to it."[4] Angels appear in every civilization and every culture, have played a major role in almost every world religion, and are far more active in human affairs than most people would suspect. Muslims claim that the "Angel Gabriel," for example, gave Muhammad the revelations in the *Koran*, which now influence over a billion Muslims.[5] So who can ignore the subject of angels?

And yet until recently in most quarters, angels *have* been ignored, even by the Christian church in whose Scriptures angels play a major role. When Billy Graham wrote his bestselling *Angels: God's Secret Agents*, he was surprised at how few books existed on the subject, and further, he reflected that he had never *once* heard a sermon preached about them.[6] Today angels are no longer ignored. In theater, television, literature, film, art, and music—and even among skeptics, who sometimes can't seem to help themselves[7]—angels are back in the popular mind.

This is all to the good for several reasons. First, angels inherently remind people of God, and of their responsibility to Him. Second, the very subject of a spiritual race of beings naturally brings to mind the deepest personal questions people have asked throughout history. If angels exist, then we are not the only form of life in the universe, and we certainly didn't evolve naturalistically from primordial interstellar gases.[8] If angels exist, a spiritual universe *must* exist, which naturally carries us back to the profound question of God as Creator, and such related questions as Who am I? Where did I come from? What is the purpose of my life? Where am I going when I die?

A final reason why angels should not be ignored is that not *all* angels are good, and people need to know this today more than ever before. In fact, the Bible suggests the number of *evil* angels is very large (Matthew 12:26; Revelation 12:3,4,7-9)—one out of every three may actually be malicious (Revelation 12:4). The Bible tells us there were rebellious angels in heaven. They chose to follow Satan and were cast from heaven with him (Luke 10:18). In the future, they will again wage "war in heaven" against the good angels. But once again, "they will not be strong enough" and "Satan . . . [will be] thrown down to the earth, and his angels . . . with him" (Revelation 12:7-9).

For most people, however, the very concept of an *evil* angel is a contradiction, like dry water or cold heat. Aren't all angels *good* by definition? But what if all aren't? Given their biblical numbers and influence, if we don't take the time to consider at least the possibility of evil angels, we may suffer for it.

In the end, when human history is over the influence of angels in this world, despite their invisibility, will probably be more obvious and certainly more profound than we suspect. As theologian J.I. Packer recently commented, "Both as communicators and as guardians their work is ordinarily unnoticeable, and not until we get to heaven shall we know how much we owe to it."[9]

Introduction

1. *Just how popular* **are** *angels today—and why?*

Recent polls indicate that almost three out of four adult
and teenage Americans believe in angels. That's about 200
million people![10] Every year, the American Conference on
Angels hold meetings to discuss the subject. There are
angel seminars, angel newsletters, college courses on
angels, and angel sections in bookstores. Besides the Hell's
Angels, "Charlie's Angels," the Angel Watch Network, and
Guardian Angels, there is the Angel Collectors Club of
America, the National Association of Angel Lovers, and
dozens of angel enterprises, such as the Angels for All
Seasons store in Denver, Angels in Heaven Day Nursery in
Cleveland, and Angel Threads, a children's boutique in
Tucson.

The December 1993 *Time* article noted earlier revealed
that five of the ten books then on the religious bestseller list
for *Publisher's Weekly* were about angels, commenting,
"This rising fascination is more popular than theological, a
grass-roots revolution of the spirit in which all sorts of
people are finding all sorts of reasons to seek answers about
angels for the first time in their lives."[11] A year later even
the NBC evening news noted the national fascination with
angels.

Angels have almost universal good press today, from the
angel "Clarence" in the popular Jimmy Stewart movie *It's a
Wonderful Life,* to the angel played by Michael Landon in
"Highway to Heaven," the recent "Touched by an Angel"
TV series, and the many recent prime-time network spe-
cials where angels are always engaged in good deeds.

With literally tens of millions of people now interested in
angels—and even open to personal contact with them—no
one can deny the importance or relevance of this topic.

Perusing a sampling of titles of recent angel books is
illuminating: *Angels on Assignment, Devotion to the Holy
Angels, 100 Ways to Attract the Angels, Send Me Your
Guardian Angel, Ask Your Angels, Angels for Your Chil-
dren, Creating with the Angels, Angels of Mercy, Messen-
gers of Light: The Angel's Guide to Spiritual Growth, Angels
Among Us, Angel Wisdom, Answers from the Angels, Angel
Voices, The Angels Within Us, Angelic Messenger Cards,
There's an Angel on Your Shoulder: Angel Encounters in
Everyday Life, A Treatise on Angel Magic, Angels and Mor-
tals: Their Co-Creative Power.* These are only a few of the
titles that could be listed, and most suggest that people are

now seeking to *commune* with angels in quite intimate ways. Today's popular angels play roles from personal friends to guidance counselors to spiritual advisers. And much more. Perhaps angels are here to stay.

But this doesn't answer the question of why angels should be so popular. There are probably several reasons. First, this generation has witnessed a dramatic spiritual revival that has included everything from Christianity to the New Age movement to the darker forms of the occult—and this has undoubtedly increased an interest in the subject of angels and spirits.

Second, there is a kind of innate fascination with the subject because of the larger implications discussed earlier.

Third, a preexisting belief system for angels is already in place from Christian, pagan, and virtually every other religious tradition. For example, most Roman Catholics are brought up to pray to their guardian angels, while major holidays like Christmas and Easter recall angel stories year after year.

Fourth, as people are increasingly searching for answers and meaning in life, angels are now thought to play a major role in providing those answers. For example, there is a growing movement which teaches people that angels reside within us already and are waiting to tap our human potential, enhance our creativity, and provide us with psychological fulfillment and spiritual self-enlightenment. Thus, promoters of angel contact offer what people want and need in troubled times: assurance, love, and guidance. They say, "The angels hold the answers to many of our questions" and, "Spiritual help is always available from the angels" or, "The angels want us to become enlightened" and, "The angels are the caretakers of our souls.... Their wonderful love [is] everywhere."[12]

Fifth, in the majority of men's minds, there is a prior assumption that angels are *only* good and therefore contacting them is also *only* good (and consequently without risk). If angels really can be contacted, why not?—and what an adventure!

Sixth, angels by definition seek to interact with humanity. The very purpose of the good angels is to help us—and the very goal of the evil angels is to deceive us.

In essence, angels are now popular because given their nature and ours, and our modern culture, it couldn't be otherwise.

Section I
The Good Angels

2. What is the meaning of the biblical words for angel?

The Hebrew word *mal'akh* and the Greek word *aggelos* both mean "messenger" and can be used of either men *or* spirits. For example, in Mark 1:2 *aggelos* is applied directly to John the Baptist, "Behold I send my messenger [*aggelos*] before your face," while *mal'akh* is used in the corresponding prophecy of Malachi 3:1.

Because the meaning of the word "angel" is simply that of "messenger," only the context can determine whether a *human* or *angelic* messenger is being referred to. In rare cases, it is difficult to determine which is meant. By far the most common use of the "angel" in the Bible is of a godly spirit messenger—what we normally think of as a good angel.

When Scripture uses the term "holy angel" or "angel," it refers to the godly and unfallen spirits created directly by God (Mark 8:38; Luke 9:26; Acts 10:22; Revelation 14:10). When it uses "Satan's angels," "evil spirits," "unclean spirits," and the like, it refers to *fallen* angels, who are the servants of Satan (Matthew 12:24; 25:41).

The word "angel" appears some 300 times in 24 books of the Bible; however, this does not include additional words that also designate angels, such as "sons of God," "holy ones," "morning stars," "cherubim," "seraphs," "ministering spirits," and "watchers." In all, the term "angel" or its equivalents are found in 35 books of the Bible.

3. What are angels?

Angels are spirit beings created by God prior to the creation of the universe (Job 38:7). They were created as servants of God, Christ, and the church to perform the will of God in the earth (Hebrews 1:6,14). Apparently innumerable, they are of various ranks and abilities, and have various duties (Revelation 5:11; 8:2; 9:15; 12:7; Ephesians 1:21; Colossians 1:16).

Angels are clearly *personal* spirits. They have personal wills (Hebrews 1:6), expressed joy at the creation of the world (Job 38:7), rejoice over a sinner's repentance (Luke 15:10), and convey concern and consternation, as when the apostle John wrongly attempted to worship an angel (Revelation 22:9). In addition, they are curious (1 Peter 1:10-12), talk to each other (Revelation 14:18), and worship and praise God (Revelation 7:11). In human form, they can communicate directly with men (Genesis 19). Angels may command other angels (Revelation 7:3; 14:17,18) or battle demons (Daniel 10:13; Revelation 12:7,8). They may appear in dreams, as to Joseph (Matthew 1:20), visibly as normal men (Genesis 18:1-8), or as beings of brightness or in shining garments (Luke 24:4). When they appear directly to men, the result is usually one of emotional shock or fear; hence, the common biblical refrain of the angels, "Fear not" (Luke 1:12; 2:10 KJV). In the Bible, only three angels are ever named: Michael, Gabriel, and Lucifer.

Angels are immortal and can never die (Luke 20:35). As we will see, they are incredibly powerful, and they have great intelligence and wisdom. They use the same measurements as humans (Revelation 21:17) and may eat either human or angelic food (Genesis 19:3; Psalm 78:23-25).

Angels apparently have spiritual bodies.[13] Although they never marry (Luke 20:35,36), this does not necessarily mean that they are without gender.

In their natural state, angels can move at tremendous speeds and are not bound by space and time in the manner we are. They can be present in great numbers in limited space; for example, seven demons simultaneously inhabited Mary Magdalene (Mark 16:9) and possibly thousands of demons may have inhabited the body of the demoniac of the Gerasenes at the same time (Luke 8:30). They can, by whatever means, be aware of things like men's prayers and future events (Luke 1:13-16). Yet despite their abilities, they have evident limits in both knowledge and power (Daniel 10:13; Matthew 24:36; 1 Peter 1:11,12; Revelation 12:7).

Morally, there are two categories of angels: the holy or elect angels (1 Timothy 5:21) and the fallen angels, who are described in the Bible as evil spirits or demons. Again, these demons are the rebellious angels who will not be redeemed (Hebrews 2:11-17) and whose final end is the lake of fire (Matthew 25:41). While some of these fallen angels are now free to roam, others are currently kept in eternal bonds (Jude 6; 2 Peter 2:4).

Different classifications among the angels include the *cherubim*, apparently the highest class of angels and having indescribable beauty and power. These angels were placed at the east of the Garden of Eden to guard the way to the tree of life after man was expelled (Genesis 3:24). They appear in connection with the dwelling place of God in the Old Testament (Exodus 25:17-22; Hebrews 9:5) and are primarily concerned with the glory and worship of God. For example, the four living creatures of Ezekiel are cherubim (Ezekiel 1:1,28; 10:4,18-22). The cherubim are never referred to as angels, although this may be because they are not specifically messengers. Their main purpose is to proclaim and protect God's glory, sovereignty, and holiness. Satan was also apparently part of the cherubim class, making his rebellion and fall all the worse. ("Cherubim" is the Hebrew plural of "cherub" [Ezekiel 28:12,14,16].)

A second class includes the *seraphim*, who are consumed with personal devotion to God (Isaiah 6:3). There are also *archangels* such as Michael, angels of yet lower rank, and special groups of angels (Revelation 1:7; 8:2; 15:1,7, etc.).

Perhaps we should mention here that a specific term, "the angel of the Lord" (*Malach-YHWH*) is used throughout the Old Testament (e.g., Genesis 22:11,12; Exodus 3:2; 2 Kings 19:35). But this term does *not* refer to a created angel. It refers to Jesus Christ. Many people think that Christ first appeared on earth only at the point of the incarnation when He was born in Bethlehem. In fact, Christ repeatedly appeared to men and is spoken of throughout the Old Testament under the name, "the angel of the Lord." The angel's identity as Christ is indicated not only by the attributes of deity He possesses, but by the fact that the Jews themselves held this angel to be the divine Messiah.[14]

Although the godly angels are considered to reside in heaven (Revelation 10:1), we are not told the nature of their specific dwelling places, if any. Of course, if angels do have spiritual bodies of some sort, this might indicate that they have fixed dwelling places (Jude 6).

4. How powerful are angels?

Angels are incredibly powerful. Peter puts the case mildly when he says they are "greater in power and might" than men (2 Peter 2:11). For example, only one angel was sent to destroy the entire city of Jerusalem (1 Chronicles 21:15), while only two angels were needed to destroy the cities of Sodom and Gomorrah and all the surrounding cities (Genesis 19:13,24,25). One angel is even able to lay hold of Satan himself to bind him for ten centuries (Revelation 20:1-3). "Destroying angels" produced the ten plagues on Egypt, including the death of all Egypt's firstborn—millions of people (Exodus 12:13,23,29-30; Psalm 78:43, 49; Hebrews 11:28). The four angels of Revelation have power over the winds of the entire earth (Revelation 7:2,3).

Other angels are indirectly associated with the destruction of one-third of the entire heavens and earth—one-third of the seas, the rivers, and the vegetation, and one-third of the sun, moon, and stars (Revelation 8,9). In Revelation 9:14,15, four angels actually destroy one-third of the earth's entire population.

At the end of the world, the angels will gather all the spirits of the saved and unsaved dead. They will gather believers at Christ's return to earth (Matthew 24:30,31), and they will gather the unbelievers for eternal judgment (Matthew 13:39-43).

Truly, angels "excel in strength" (Psalm 103:20). But what is perhaps most amazing for the simple believer in Christ is that God tells us that we will one day judge and perhaps rule angels themselves (1 Corinthians 6:2-3)!

5. What are some popular but false ideas about good angels?

Given the degree of biblical ignorance concerning angels in our culture, as well as the revival of the New Age movement, cults, and the occult, it is not unexpected that false concepts about angels have arisen. Among these erroneous beliefs are the following: 1) that angels are the human dead; that is, that we become angels at death; 2) that angels perform God's work through various occult activities and practices; 3) that the devil *isn't* a fallen angel, or that Jesus Christ was *only* an angel; and 4) that simply because they *are* angels, all angels can be trusted to be good. Obviously this last item discounts the fact that perhaps one-third of the angels rebelled against God and are now evil spirits whose sole purpose is to accomplish the will of the devil.

These kinds of false beliefs indicate it is especially important to ascertain what Scripture does and does not teach about both the good angels and the evil angels.

6. What do good angels actually do in the Bible?

The angels who were created by God and Christ (Nehemiah 9:6; Colossians 1:16) and who did not rebel with Lucifer (Nehemiah 9:6; Colossians 1:16) exist primarily for God and Christ and thus have their lives centered on them. They worship and serve God and Christ (Philippians 2:9-11; Hebrews 1:6). They glorify and celebrate the praises of God and Christ (Job 38:7; Psalm 148:2; Isaiah 6:3; Luke 2:13,14; Revelation 5:11,12; 7:11,12). They delight to communicate the will of God and Christ, and they delight in obeying God and Christ. In *all* that they do, they *honor* God and Christ (Daniel 8:16,17; 9:21-23; 10:11; 12:6,7; Psalm 103:20; Matthew 2:13,20; 6:10; Luke 1:19,28; Acts 5:20; 8:26; 10:5; 27:23; Revelation 1:1).

They execute the purposes of God and Christ on the earth, including the governing and judging of the earth (Numbers 22:22; Psalm 103:19-21; Matthew 13:39-42; 28:2; John 5:4; Revelation 5:2; 2 Samuel 24:16; 2 Kings 19:35; Psalm 35:5,6; Acts 12:23; Revelation 16:1). For example, they were active in establishing the Mosaic law of God in the Old Testament (Acts 7:38,53; Galatians 3:19; Hebrews 2:2) and perform the judgments of Christ in the New Testament (2 Thessalonians 1:7,8; Revelation 7–9).

In performing the will of God and Christ, they are also ministering spirits to both believer and unbeliever, especially the former (1 Kings 19:5; Psalm 68:17; 104:4; Luke 16:22; Acts 12:7-11; 27:23; Hebrews 1:14). They guide, provide, encourage, and deliver God's people (Matthew 1:20; 28:5-7; Genesis 21:17-20; 1 Kings 19:5-7; 2 Kings 6:15-17; Daniel 6:20-23; 10:10-12; Acts 5:17-20; 12: 5-10). They are sent to answer prayer (Daniel 9:20-24; Acts 12:1-17; Revelation 8:4) and attend the righteous dead (Luke 16:22; Jude 9). They also protect God's people (Psalm 34:7; 35:4,5; Isaiah 63:9) and may preach to and warn the unbeliever (Revelation 14:6,7). They interpret divine visions (Zechariah 4:1; 5:5; 6:5; Daniel 7:15-27; 8:13-26) and prophesy concerning the future (Daniel 9:20-27, 10:1-21; Revelation 1:1; 22:6,8). Further, they can control the forces of nature (Revelation 7:1; 16:3,8-9) and even influence nations (Daniel 10:13,21; 12:1; Revelation 12:7-9; 13:1-7; 16:13,14).

However, in the Bible, the angels are most conspicuous in association with the Person and work of Jesus Christ. They announced the conception of Christ, the birth of Christ, the resurrection of Christ, and His ascension and second coming. They protected and strengthened Christ at His temptation; they know and delight in the gospel of Christ and execute the purposes of Christ. They will attend and accompany Him at His return, and they will gather all men, good and evil, for the final judgment of Christ (Matthew 1:20,21; 2:13-15; 4:11; 13:39-43; 16:17; 24:31; 25:31; 28:5-7; Luke 2:10-12; 22:43; John 1:51; 5:22-29; Acts 1:11; Ephesians 3:9,10; 2 Thessalonians 1:7; 1 Timothy 3:6; 1 Peter 1:12).

What is perhaps most relevant is that what the good angels are said to do biblically is exactly the *opposite* of what we find the popular angels (the term we are using for those beings who are, in reality, evil angels or demons) doing today. Biblically, the good angels do their work for God and then disappear. But these popular angels act like modern spirit guides. They do not worship Christ; they deny Him and distort His teachings. They reject God's will and rebel against it by seeking to prevent men's salvation.

When we examine the godly angels, we see that their proclamations support God's purposes; their miracles support God's interests; their preaching is proven to communicate God's will. Their love of Christ is proven throughout Scripture and by what they do today. In ministering to God's children, they remind them of God's love and care for them (Matthew 18:10; Psalm 34:7; 91:11,12; Daniel 6:22). Also, their character is proven wise and holy by their refusal to be worshiped by men (Colossians 2:18; Revelation 19:10; 22:9) and by the fact that their worship and devotion is given solely to God and Christ.

But with many of the popular angels of today, it is another story entirely, as we will see in Section II.

7. What do good angels do today, and how they might touch our lives?

A number of contemporary books recount stories of the holy angels in the lives of people throughout history and today. These stories are truly encouraging and inspiring. These angels have saved the lives of genuine Christians, provided encouragement in times of persecution, and facilitated the conversion of non-Christians.[15] Consider a few examples.

In *A Rustle of Angels*, evangelical Christian Marilynn Webber relates her story, first published in the December 1992 *Ladies' Home Journal*. One day, despondent over circumstances, she was walking home near some railroad tracks. Slowly crossing over them, she suddenly realized an oncoming train was so close that she could see the blue eyes and the terrified face of the engineer. But she was paralyzed with fear. However, instead of being struck instantaneously, she was miraculously pushed from the tracks as if by a giant hand, even though "no one was there! There was not a person in sight!"[16] She survived, to say the least, with a renewed interest in angels!

In *Celebration of Angels*, we find other stories of deliverance. For example, Walt Shepard was a very depressed non-Christian who decided to take his own life: He rammed his Sunbeam sports car at 120 miles an hour into what he thought was an abandoned car on the side of the road. The car exploded, and both vehicles caught on fire. If the car's driver and passenger had not been outside of the vehicle resting, they would have been killed instantly.

Walt went through the windshield and landed in the car's engine area with fire surrounding him. Trapped there, he passed out. Even though the heat was so intense no one could get close enough to help, police officers watched in amazement as two men suddenly appeared, pulled him out of the fire, held him, and helped the ambulance attendants place him in the ambulance. The police and a Holiday Inn manager "all confirmed that two figures walked up to the car as though there were no fire at all. People said the searing heat kept everybody else 50 to 100 feet back. The attending police were dumbstruck by the peculiar rescue."[17] Although Walt nearly died and had many painful months of hospitalization in a body cast, he realized he could have been saved only by angels. It was obvious; he now *knew* God wanted him to live. The result of his experience was his acceptance of Christ as his personal Lord and Savior.

Other stories are recounted where Christians have heard warning voices telling them not to do something or not to go somewhere—advice which they later discovered had saved their lives.[18,19]

Then there is the story of David Moore and his friend Henry Gardner, trapped in a small plane in severe fog with only a few minutes of fuel left. They radioed to the Asheville, North Carolina, airport for emergency instructions but were informed the field was closed due to fog and that the airport had no instrument capability for emergency landing. The pilots were instructed to return to Greenville and land there.

Henry notified the tower that there was insufficient fuel to return to Greenville and that they must land now. There was a period of silence. A voice then told them that they could land and that emergency preparations would be undertaken. The airport controller then gave them *specific* and *detailed* instructions, which soon allowed the plane to land in an otherwise impossible situation. In a shaky voice, Henry thanked the air traffic controller for saving their lives. Another silence. The controller responded, "What are you talking about? We lost all radio contact with you when we told you to return to Greenville." "You *what*?" Henry asked, incredulous. "We never heard from you again, and we never heard you talking to us or to anyone else," the controller told them. "We were stunned when we saw you break through the clouds."

The Asheville control tower had never given the pilots permission to land, because it *couldn't*—it was incapable of guiding them safely to the ground.[20]

Hundreds of stories like these are recounted in modern angel literature. Although many lives are saved, many more are obviously not. Why God helps some and not others must be left to His wisdom. But clearly, the angels are more active in our world than most people suspect. Like Elisha's servant, if the veil were removed, the average American would be stunned (2 Kings 6:15-17).

Angels can touch our lives at any moment. We can rest assured that should angelic intervention be necessary to fulfill God's purposes, it *will* happen.

8. Does everyone have a guardian angel?

Although Scripture does not explicitly state that everyone has a guardian angel, many commentators feel that this could be true, at least for believers. Certainly, given the innumerable number of the angels and God's love for His own people, it would be a logical conclusion. Scripturally, it appears that children, at least, do have guardian angels (Matthew 18:10).

Whether or not every believer has one, there are certainly what can only be termed "guardian angels"—those angels whom God sends at specific times to guard, encourage, and protect His own people. Of course, this may also occur among unbelievers when it suits God's purposes. Obviously, many nonbelievers who will yet come to faith in Christ may face personal crises or life-threatening situations that require angelic intervention if these people are going to survive in order to *become* Christians (see Hebrews 1:14).

But the issue here is not whether Christians or even many nonbelievers have guardian angels. Our concern is the emphasis in modern angel literature that all people *do* have guardian angels whom they are specifically *to contact* for regular instruction and spiritual guidance. As Terry Lynn Taylor and Mary Beth Crain state in their daily devotional inspired by the popular "angels": "Everyone has a guardian angel;" and, "When God looks at you, God sees two beings: you and your guardian angel. Your guardian angel is your spiritual traveling companion through life.... Your guardian angel knows what you came here to do.... Getting to know your guardian angel will help you to get to know yourself."[21-25]

Section II

Modern Angel Encounters: The Popular Angels

9. What does it mean for us today that Satan and his demons were once holy angels who fell from their heavenly position of glory?

The biblical truth that some angels are now evil beings means that spiritual discernment is not a luxury but a necessity today. In an era of worldwide occult revival, no one should attempt the phenomenon of "contacting angels," "channeling angels," developing "angel consciousness," or the like. All these are merely ruses by the fallen evil angels (demons) to hide their true purposes.

How do we know the popular angels are not who they claim to be? Because the angels who remained faithful to God are holy and godly in their behavior; the entities behind the modern angelic revelations are neither. Godly angels glorify Christ and do not give revelations contrary to Scripture as the popular angels do. Biblical angels characteristically operate "behind the scenes." The popular angels are more than willing to operate in the open and to communicate in spiritistic fashion. The end result of the actions of godly angels will bring honor to God; for evil angels, it will result in spiritual deception.[26]

In essence, good angels do their job and then vanish. They never stick around in the occult tradition of spirit guides or give messages that run contrary to scriptural doctrine or ethics.

10. Exactly who are the evil angels, what are some false ideas concerning them, and what are their powers?

According to the Bible, the evil angels are morally corrupted spirits in rebellion against God (Psalm 106:37; John 8:44; 2 Peter 2:4; James 2:19; Jude 6). Their rebellion was instituted under the leadership of Satan (Jude 6; 1 John 3:8; Matthew 12:24,25; 25:41; Ezekiel 28:12-17) and resulted in their expulsion from heaven (Luke 10:18; cf. Revelation 12:7-9). As a result they became destructive, self-centered creatures who seek to thwart the purposes of God and

Christ (Deuteronomy 32:17; Psalm 106:37; Revelation 2:10; 1 Peter 5:8; Ephesians 6:11; Matthew 13:39; Luke 22:31; 1 Thessalonians 2:18; 1 Timothy 4:1; Mark 3:11; 4:15).

One of the demon's principal concerns is to deceive people through false religion and/or deceptive miracles and thereby to blind them to spiritual truth (2 Corinthians 4:4; Acts 26:18; 2 Corinthians 11:14; 2 Thessalonians 2:9,10; Revelation 16:14; 20:10).

Demons are forever set in their ways, know their eternal destiny, and have no opportunity for redemption. Thus, they will eventually be cast forever into the lake of fire (Matthew 25:41; Revelation 20:2,3,7-10). This would seem to explain why they responded to Jesus with fear and derision, saying, "What do I have to do with You, Jesus, Son of the Most High God?" (Mark 5:7; cf., Luke 4:41) and, "Have You come here to torment us before the time?" (Matthew 8:29).

Demons are not the spirits of dead men or a pre-Adamite race, as some people argue, for the spirits of the human dead are not free to roam (Luke 16:19-31; 2 Peter 2:9). Nor are they merely personifications of evil or of natural forces (such as the "gods" of nature), as skeptics assume. Nor are demons the superstitious designation for particular natural diseases such as epilepsy or mental illness. Scripture clearly distinguishes these disorders from demon possession, although it is possible that both can be present or that demon possession could induce mental illness.[27]

If we were to catalog the powers and abilities of angels given in Scripture, we would gain a glimpse into their capabilities, and hence also discern the abilities of demons as corrupted angels. However, it must never be forgotten that demons are creatures who are ultimately constrained by the sovereign power and purpose of God. When needed, the Christian has power over them (1 John 4:4; James 4:7) because Christ Himself was victorious over Satan at the cross (Hebrews 2:14; Colossians 2:15; John 12:31). Jesus proved His complete power over demons (Matthew 12:28; Mark 1:34), often casting demons out of people (Matthew 8:31; 15:22-28), and He commanded His disciples to do the same (Mark 6:13; Matthew 10:1; Luke 10:17).

11. What do evil angels do today, how are they contacted, and how may they touch our lives?

The listing of demonic power given in the Bible is surprisingly relevant for what demons actually do today. For example, as we documented in detail in *The Coming Darkness* and other books, evil angels (demons) *imitate* good angels and express great concern for people's welfare; they also give false visions and revelations in dreams or through channeling, automatic writing, etc. They can possess people, perform various miracles, cause insanity, or commit murder. They can produce various physical ailments, sicknesses, or torments. They can predict the future, encourage occult practices, and manipulate the human mind by impressing thoughts, ideas, or images upon it. They can influence nature. They seek to be worshiped, to pervert God's ways, and they can even assume any physical form at will, from human to child, animal to mythological creature. In the end, in general, they destroy people's lives.

The methods used by the evil angels to make contact with people are typically those found in the world of the occult—through altered states of consciousness, psychic abilities, methods of divination, drugs, magic ritual, and the like. Basically, the desire and commitment on the part of someone to personally contact angels or spirits by inviting them into one's life is all that is needed. For example, "Sometimes all it takes to establish communication is the thought of an angel or the desire to connect with one.... Pick an angel to attune to. Have some writing paper nearby in case a message comes through that you want to record."[28] Or, "Call a prayer meeting with the angels. Invite your guardian angel, or any angels you like, to join with you. Pray in any way you like, and be aware of any images, words, and ideas that come to you."[29]

Perhaps the most recommended method for establishing contact is meditation. Here, one seeks to enter a unitive or a noncognitive, "empty" state of consciousness.[30] As the author of *Messengers of Light: The Angel's Guide to Spiritual Growth* states: "There are a variety of approaches to meditation, such as focusing on a mantra, on imagery, or on physical objects, or simply paying attention to one's breathing.... You may want to use the word *angel* as a form of mantra.... The messages may not come to you in words; often angels speak to you with feelings and images.... Centering [focused attention; occult "alignment"] is a way of synchronizing our energy.... [which connects] with our higher self and with the angels who guide us."[31]

Prayer and the creation of an "angel altar" are two additional popular methods to establish contact.[32] For example, "angels love candlelight. Candlelight illuminates and purifies the atmosphere and attracts angels. After you have created your altar or shrine, light the candle and sit quietly in front of it. Draw in the beauty and ask the angels to join you."[33]

Because they are relatively easy to contact for those determined to do so, evil angels can touch people's lives today in an almost innumerable variety of ways. Before we turn to specifics, it is important to look at one simple, but crucial, fact:

12. Do the popular angels deny key biblical teachings? Can holy angels possibly deny Christ's teachings?

The godly angels would never deny the teachings of Jesus Christ and the Bible. Yet the popular angels do this as a matter of routine. Consider a few examples: "God is the totality of your living experience"[34]; "God is life. You and God share the same bed, the same car, the same glass of water. You and God are one."[35,36]

The popular angels teach basic pagan, New Age beliefs including Hinduism, occult practice, pantheism (all is God, God is all), universalism, and the idea that Christ dwells within all people, irrespective of their faith in Him.[37]

Yet these "angels" also make simple errors of fact in both theological and nontheological areas.[38] Consider the following from *Angel Wisdom*: "The angels do not judge"; "Our true selves are angelic"; "All religions . . . worship the same God"; "Our souls remain in a pure state of innocence"; and "Consider the possibility that ultimately everything is true [see 1 John 2:21]."[39]

As people consider their involvement with angels today, they should realize that good angels will never tell lies. The remainder of our discussion will prove that the popular angels are not who they claim.

13. Are the popular angels active in cults? What are some false Christian approaches to angels?

Most people would be surprised to know that literally scores of modern cults and new religions were instituted and/or nurtured by "angelic" contact. Consider a few examples. As we documented thoroughly in *Everything You Ever Wanted to Know About Mormonism*, no religion is more anti-Christian than the Mormon faith. Yet who was it who led Mormon founder Joseph Smith to the alleged "gold plates" from which the *Book of Mormon* was occultly translated but the "angel Moroni"?[40] Mormon history is replete with angelic guidance, direction, and revelation.

As we documented in *The Facts on the Jehovah's Witnesses*, "angels" have played a major role in the Jehovah's Witness religion and even in the terribly biased translation of their Bible, *The New World Translation*.

The noted seventeenth-century medium Emanuel Swedenborg also routinely contacted angels and eventually formed another pervasively anti-Christian sect, *The Church of the New Jerusalem*, sometimes termed the New Church or Swedenborgian faith. Swedenborg's angels were with him constantly, whispering, teaching, impressing thoughts and ideas into his mind.[41]

Anthroposophy (a combination of theosophy and gnostic Christianity) is another illustration of an extremely anti-Christian sect begun with the help of angels. Its founder, Rudolph Steiner, was heavily influenced by Swedenborg. Steiner contacted the dead and other spirits, including angels, whom he described in detail in his writings and lectures. He taught that every person had a guardian angel throughout their many incarnations on earth.[42]

Jose Silva is the founder of the eight-million-member Silva Mind Control (SMC) religion. Its purpose is to allow people to contact "inner advisers" for information and guidance. SMC was started when Silva contacted an "angel" during "astral projection" who proceeded to give him the principles of Silva Mind Control.[43]

Other examples could be given, including the Self Realization Fellowship founded by Paramahansa Yogananda and the Unity School of Christianity founded by Charles and Myrtle Fillmore.[44] But obviously the angels who helped begin or influenced such anti-Christian religious systems could not have been the good angels because the revelations they gave are as antibiblical as can be found. Any perusal of the literature of these groups, especially their theological literature, proves this. Yet all these religions actually either *claim* to be Christian or claim not to be contrary to the Christian faith. As a result, they have confused some Christians who have accepted their teachings.

But there are many other ways in which deceiving spirits have infiltrated the church. The dramatic increase in the number of books advocating angel contact began many years ago with the late Reverend Roland Buck's *Angels on Assignment*. Characteristically, however, this text had little to do with the holy angels. The content of Buck's book and an examination of the history behind it, including the fact that the "angels'" original statements were changed to make them consistent with biblical teaching, indicates that Buck was not a participant in godly angelic revelation, but in a spiritistic deception. Regardless of Buck's and publisher Charles and Francis Hunter's evident sincerity in publishing the book, the "angels'" teachings, as always, revealed their true nature.[45]

One issue of *The Christian Parapsychologist* (a journal seeking to integrate Christianity and the occult) was devoted entirely to angels. It included five articles—one each by a psychic, a Swedenborgian, a nature mystic, an anthroposophist, and a Jungian. In "Some Thoughts About Angels," J. Dover Wellman, vicar of Emmanuel Church and author of *A Priest's Psychic Diary*, says the following. In common with Mormonism and Swedenborgianism, he lumps virtually all spirits into the category of deceased humans and encourages various occult methods to contact "angels":

> I believe spiritual entities are all around us.... In this matter of our realizing the presence of the angels, the initiative always lies with them as superior beings.... Jesus Christ was, I believe, one of these pre-existent angelic beings.... His purpose in dwelling on earth was to inform us of our own potentiality as beings who could be restored to "angelhood"....
>
> When the state of trance frees our spirit-soul from our body-soul, we act as pure spirit. Our extra-sensory perceptions function more efficiently, making known to us that which is otherwise hidden.... We are ourselves then approaching the level of the life of the angels.... In this condition ... our communion with them would be enhanced and their influence upon us much increased.[46]

Other authors in that same issue of *The Christian Parapsychologist* agree. Brian Kingslake is a minister of the New Church, based on the spiritistic revelations given to Emanuel Swedenborg. He is the author of *Swedenborg Explores the Spiritual Dimension*. In his article "A Heaven of Angels from the Human Race," he accepts the common mediumistic and Swedenborgian teaching that "all the millions of spirits inhabiting the spiritual world—angels and devils alike—are *human beings* who once inhabited this earth, or some other earth in the material universe." He proceeds to argue that God's alleged purpose is to "form a heaven of angels from the human race."[47]

Dorothy Maclean is a New Age leader and cofounder of the spiritistic Findhorn community in Scotland, as well as the author of several books on how to contact angels and other spirits. In "Angels Today," she says of her personal experience with angels: "I found that I could not make contact with these angels until I myself was in a state of consciousness similar to theirs.... To them we had magnificent divine potentials.... We were gods in the making.... They await our choice to let our lives be guided by our intuitions, by our angelic awareness, that we may cooperate with them."[48]

In "The Hierarchies Regained," anthroposophical student Evelyn Capel, a minister in Rudolph Steiner's so-called Christian Community and author of *The Tenth Hierarchy*, further encourages the interaction of "angels" and humanity along occult lines.[49]

Finally, in "Angels and Archetypes," Christopher Bryant, a priest in the Society of St. John the Evangelist and long-time student of occult psychologist Carl Jung, observes, "It is probable that all unknowingly we benefit by the ministry of angels who do their work in the unconscious levels of the mind which are in touch with the psychic world."[50]

There are many other examples. The popular late preacher William Branham claimed to speak for God. But throughout his life he was guided by lying spirits (his "angels"), who would whisper to him and, apparently, occultly "heal" many people each year. Despite his vast influence in Pentecostalism, he was a false prophet who denied the true nature of God. For example, he once said, "Trinitarianism [belief in the Trinity] is of the devil! I say that [with the authority of] THUS SAITH THE LORD."[51]

The Rev. Edward W. Oldring is the author of *I Work with Angels* and *I Walk and Talk with Angels*. The "angels" supposedly appeared to him in order to assist him in "preparing many [Christian] people...to work with God's angels...and to...cooperate with...the angels."[52] Therefore, he teaches, "There is a spiritualism [contact with spirits] that is ordained of God.... It is part of God's plan."[53] However, the angels that speak to him blatantly give false interpretations of the Bible and therefore could not possibly be the godly angels.[54]

Consider a final illustration. G. Don Gilmore is the minister of Plymouth Congregational Church in Spokane, Washington, and host of the daily radio program "Perspective on Living." He has authored *Angels, Angels Everywhere*, a book on "angelic" contact. His book is an illustration not only of the potential disguising of spiritism but also of the normalizing and internalizing or "psychologizing" of spiritistic experience. For Gilmore, "angel contact" encompasses a wide range of phenomena. For example, it includes the occult concept of "thought forms"—spiritual manifestations allegedly constructed mentally from psychic energy. Thus:

I believe that angels are forms, images, and expressions through which the essences and energy forces of God can be transmitted and that, since there are an infinite number of these forms, the greatest service anyone can pay the angelic host is never consciously to limit the ways angels might appear to us.[55]

Of course, at this point, the doors have swung open to accepting virtually all forms of supernatural occult phenomena. Every religious/spiritistic manifestation today claims to be associated with "divine" energy or the "energy forces of God." In fact, Gilmore claims that "God's energy" is behind not only the traditional angelic manifestations in various world religions, but much more as well.

One of Gilmore's principal concerns is the development of what he terms "angel consciousness." This is basically a euphemism for psychic development, "higher consciousness," and/or spirit possession.[56-58] Thus, "angel consciousness" simply involves an altered state of consciousness and/or openness to the psychic realm, which is then interpreted as involvement with divine energies and powers. One develops "angel consciousness" by means of, for example, creative visualization, which supposedly opens the doors to "the moving streams of unlimited energy."[59,60]

Because God's essential "energy forms" are allegedly everywhere, we are told it is the Christian's responsibility to establish contact with them for spiritual growth. In common with much occultism, Gilmore suggests that we can actually "raise" angels through the powers of our own consciousness, much as the occult magician attempts to raise spirits or demons through the circle of power in his ritual.[61] Quoting popular occultist Dion Fortune, Gilmore also interprets angelic contact as communion with our "higher self":

Could it be that the highest and best angel form is not external to us but one's own best and truest self? Dion Fortune once wrote.... "The Holy Guardian Angel, be it remembered, is really our own high self." ... Add to the Outer Self, Self One, the inner body—intuition, genius, sixth sense, ESP, psychic power, inner knowing—and you might have more angel forms to use in your creative work.[62]

Gilmore tells readers that personal contact with angels is easy: "You will be amazed at how often you will make contact with the energy essence of the angel form."[63] He also encourages positive mental affirmations to facilitate the process of angel consciousness and contact, such as: "God and God's helpers are never far away.... The Light of God surrounds me.... The Power of God protects me.... Wherever I am, God is!"[64]

In conclusion, Gilmore's "angel" contact encompasses a wide variety of forms of psychic development, spiritism, and occult manifestations. Thus, it could hardly involve contact with godly angels, or involve doing the will of God, who prohibits occult involvement (Deuteronomy 18:9-12).

14. How do popular angels support the world of the occult?

It would be impossible to provide even the briefest survey of the manner in which the popular angels promote the world of the occult. In *Angel Wisdom* we find the encouragement to use mantras and mandalas; to explore shamanistic vision quests; to contact one's power animal (a spirit guide who appears in the form of an animal); and to pursue psychic healing and the manipulation of chakras.[65] In *Angelic Messenger Cards*, we find people guided to accept contacting the dead.[66] In *Creating with the Angels*, we find dreamwork: "Dream time is spirit time and offers a great opportunity to play with the angels.... Allow the angels to help you interpret your dreams."[67] In *The Angels Within Us*, we find angels taking people deep into altered states of consciousness in order to establish contact with them.[68] These "angels" also support New Age medicine and occult holistic health practices and occult religions such as theosophy.[69,70]

The popular angels also encourage the practice of necromancy or contacting the dead for divination, as well as various forms of occult magic.[71,72]

The popular angels often encourage the development of practices like automatic writing, dictation, or speaking to get their messages published and in circulation.[73] For example, Karen Goldman, author of *Angel Voices* and *The Angel Book*, believes that "the angels are directing and guiding her writing." (*Angel Voices*, back cover flap). She used the "Sedona Method RELEASE Technique" from the Sedona Institute in Arizona to contact her "inner angel" who now guides her writing.[74] Sally Sharp, author of *100 Ways to Attract the Angels*, was also led into automatic writing by her angels, as were many other angel authors.[75,76]

Rosemary Ellen Guiley, author of *Angels of Mercy* and many books on occult and mystical topics, such as *The*

Encyclopedia of Witches and Witchcraft and *Harper's Encyclopedia of Mystical and Paranormal Experiences*, recalls that her life has been directed by unseen presences, which she interprets as angels who have guided her specifically into this area:

> For many years, I have felt the presence of guiding beings in my life.... My initial intuitive sense was that these helping beings were "angels," and that is what I have always called them.... I sense a small group of angels who are around me all the time, connected to my personal and professional lives. They are joined by other angels who come and go depending on circumstances.... When I began work on *Angels of Mercy* the angels came out in force. It seemed I had a small army looking over my shoulder to weigh in with their various influences.... In addition to my writing, I lecture a great deal, and I feel the guiding presence of a "speaking angel"... I sense his presence. He is a facilitator who helps me organize and deliver talks.[77]

The name of her "speaking angel" is Plato, and he does in fact speak through her—just like many prominent spiritual leaders today, including Ram Dass, the late William Branham, and others. Guiley states:

> As I began my talk, I felt a distinct shift in my consciousness, as though part of me were displaced to one side. In addition, I could feel the weight of an invisible presence on my shoulders, as though a being perched there.... I talked for two hours without looking at a single note, and got rave comments from the audience. "You don't know it, but you're a born teacher!"... As time has gone on, I have been increasingly aware of this shift in consciousness when I deliver a talk. Occasionally, someone who is clairvoyant will come up to me afterward and ask me if I know I have an angel or a being standing off to one side of me. "Yes," I say, "that's my speaking angel!"[78]

What all this means is that a good deal—and perhaps a majority—of the popular angel literature is actually from the popular angels themselves.

In fact, what field of the occult is *not* infiltrated by fallen angels? Astrology and other forms of divination, ceremonial magic, mediumism and seances, witchcraft and satanism, psychic development, shamanism—all are literally over-run with fallen angels and their deceptions. As the *Harper's Encyclopedia of Mystical and Paranormal Experience* observes, "In New Age, occult and religious beliefs, angels have made a comeback in popularity. They are portrayed in karmic aspects of astrology, channeled, meditated upon, and said to exist in spirit realms. Angelic forces are invoked in magic rituals and various magical systems and witchcraft. The popular view holds that angels are benevolent beings and are different from demons."[79]

Indeed, this is the primary goal of the demons who imitate godly angels—to confuse people as to their sphere of operation. If people can be convinced that the realm of the occult is actually the realm of angelic manifestations, they will be much more willing to experiment. And, of course, if no one knows what an angel really is, any spirit claiming to be one can seem credible. Thus, large numbers of people who contact angels today are slowly but surely being led directly into the realms of the occult.[80]

These "angels" specifically hope to reach children. For example, the author of *The Circle of Angels* was taken over by a spirit who announced through her by automatic writing, "I am the archangel Michael and together we will save the children."[81] The end result was the series of "Little Angel Books," which attempts to help children personally call upon angels through occult meditation.

15. What about popular angels and the modern channeling phenomenon?

Channeling spirit guides is now a multibillion dollar industry in the United States. But channeling angels is no different than channeling spirit guides. In both cases, one is possessed by a control spirit just as if one were a medium. This similarity is also evidenced by the fact that the messages and phenomena found in angel channeling and those found in mediumism are essentially the same.[82]

Consider the ease with which channeled spirits and angels are linked in the popular literature: "We all have spiritual guides, *angels* who take us to higher levels of consciousness and knowledge.... Our guides may take on physical presence in a dream, during meditation, or in the form of a spiritual advisor or teacher whom we may unexpectedly encounter.... I am open to my spiritual guides, and I greet them with excitement, respect, wonder, and love."[83]

Consider an illustration. Catholic Roseann Cervelli claims to have been channeling *angels* for over a decade from her home in Martinsville, New Jersey. Some of her channeled revelations were published in *Voices of Love*. How did this begin? After being raised a Catholic and developing a "strong sense of spirituality," she studied the trance revelations of medium Edgar Cayce and the methods of psychic healing, and pursued "Christ consciousness." Eventually she received the laying on of hands from a Catholic priest who became her spiritual mentor. When he laid his hands upon her, she experienced a kind of psychic opening: "After that, for the next year or so, I studied with the priest and other like-minded people. I would have a kind of mystical experience. I would be pulled into a oneness and meditative state.... These were my first experiences with the spiritual energies—very loving and very embracing."[84]

Eventually she met a medium who channeled a spirit named "Matthew." After taking the occult advice of "Matthew," Cervelli progressed to a form of psychic revelation in which she would receive energy through her head. Automatic writing then developed, which finally produced *Voices of Love*. After "Matthew," she met another spirit named "Elliott," and finally a new entity who introduced itself saying, "My name is John, and I have come to teach you about self-love." When "Matthew," "Elliott," and "John" decided to leave, they told Roseann that she would now be indwelt by a group of *angels*—and she has been channeling "angels" ever since.[85]

Now really, how could she possibly tell the difference? Especially when the revelations were the same?

Among the standard messages the "angels" want to give people is to inform them that "we are not separate from God. We *are* God.... Not only is God inside of us, but he *is* us."[86] Obviously, no godly angels are going to encourage people to adopt pantheistic beliefs that undermine the very essence of the Christian faith.

16. What about popular angels, Mary, the Pope, and Roman Catholicism?

Like most nonbiblical religions,[87] Roman Catholicism has a long tradition of accepting angelic visitations. A common Catholic "prayer to your guardian angel," which all devout Catholics learn, reads, "Angel of God, my guardian dear, to whom his love commits me here, ever this day (night) be at my side, to light and guard, to rule and guide. Amen."[88]

Officially, the Catholic church teaches that every person on earth has a guardian angel, and "devotion to one's guardian angel is encouraged."[89]

In fact, the Catholic church is becoming more interested. The Opus Sanctorum Angelorum (Work of the Holy Angels) of the Catholic Order of the Holy Cross is now accepted as an "institute recognized by the Church." Even Pope John Paul II has expressed a personal interest in angels.[90]

Many of the current books on angels are written by Catholics. In *Where Angels Walk*, the *New York Times* best-seller, Catholic Joan Anderson encourages a form of angel contact and prayers to angels. She states that "most Catholics believe that everyone receives a guardian angel at birth, a life companion especially suited to one's unique personality. Catholic children learn a comforting little prayer to initiate 'conversation' with their angel and the feast day of guardian angels is celebrated on October 2."[91]

Books such as W. Doyle Gulligan's (ed.) *Devotion to the Holy Angels* (Lumen Christi, 1990) and Catholic organizations such as the Opus Sanctorum Angelorum cited earlier (devoted to explaining and encouraging devotion to angels) prove that Catholic believers provide a ready-made audience susceptible to the popular angel phenomenon.[92] Spiritist and popular angel author Terry Lynn Taylor also argues that Catholic Marian devotion is connected with the resurgence of angels: "Mary, the Mother of Christ, is often referred to as the Queen of angels. Mary is touching the lives of those involved in angel consciousness in a deep way.... That is why ... the angels are so prevalent now."[93] The result, however, is that the revelations given by Mary (and the angels not infrequently associated with her) uniformly support Catholic theology and teachings that are antibiblical.[94] For example, the occult Marian apparitions at Medjugorje, Yugoslavia, include the appearances of *putti* or child angels, and the message they give denies the teachings of Christ.[95]

17. Why would popular angels be interested in supporting the environmental movement?

Environmental radicalism has now become a national concern, the result of overzealous activists and politicians whose sometimes misguided ways have done considerably more harm to the environment than good.[96]

But one also finds a deep concern with the environment in most spiritist writings, including those from among Native Americans, UFO contactees, New Age channelers and from modern angel revelations. The spirits' interest in this case, however, is the promotion of pantheism and nature worship—not a cleaner environment.

Environmental revelations from the "angels" teach the sacred importance of the environment and how people must be more concerned with the earth as their spiritual "parent." According to these revelations, people must learn to view the earth as divine and realize that worship of the creation is crucial to a renewed spirituality. Of course, all this reflects an increasing return to pagan nature worship (where the earth itself is divinized into a goddess) and to animism (where trees, plants, rocks, etc., are believed to contain living spirits). That even Vice President Al Gore's book on the environment encourages a pagan approach is merely an unfortunate symptom of the times.[97]

The "angels" who speak through one angel channeler emphasize, "The larger level of healing we speak of involves healing the relationship between your spirit and the spirit of the Earth.... Planet Earth has a life purpose, as you do.... Your desire to seek a deeper exchange with Nature encourages her spirit and further balances all levels of life."[98]

The popular angels also endorse a pantheistic *Gaia* concept, "Your spirit's purpose is to facilitate cooperation between you and Gaia, the Earth.... As you awaken your love as a planetary being.... it will ultimately be the means of healing Earth."[99]

Examples of animism can be seen in the following angelic revelations: "Trees have guardian spirits, and we can learn many things from sitting quietly near a tree and communicating with its energy"[100] and, "The Water Spirits are the guardian angels of natural sources of water.... All Water Spirits can teach us about our inner feelings. In learning to connect with them, we can gain many benefits."[101]

The spiritistic Findhorn community in Scotland, with its worship of nature spirits (devas) and angels, is one example of how the angels' emphasis on environmentalism leads to direct contact with demons under the guise of harmony with Mother Earth. In return for their prayers and for worship to the spirits inside trees, plants, and rivers, the angels promise people physical, emotional, and spiritual healing—along with the promise that the earth itself will evolve into perfection.[102]

18. What examples illustrate how the popular angels distort the Bible?

Perhaps the most consistent characteristic of the popular angels' approach to religion, besides inspiring false religion, is their distortion of the Bible. Obviously, if these were godly angels—especially angels who took part in the giving of the law of God, and who respect and honor Him—they could not possibly distort His Word. Demons, of course, would. For example, in *The Angels Within Us*, Scripture is universally misinterpreted to *support* the occult in violation of clear biblical prohibitions *against* the occult (e.g., Deuteronomy 18:9-12). Thus, the angels' interpretation of Matthew 5:14 is twisted to teach pantheism and the idea that we are "the creative power of the universe"; 2 Chronicles 20:17 is a "coded message" that "describes what happens when you take on the energy of [the] angel"; Psalm 91:11 is reinterpreted to encourage spiritism; John 15:1-11 is distorted to mean that we are to abide within the God-self within us, the occult "I AM Presence."[103]

In offering these teachings, the angels actually direct their contacts to read these Scriptures *in the Bible*, and then they proceed to *misinterpret* them to their listeners.[104] As angel channeler and New Age leader John Randolph Price comments, "The angels are extremely practical in showing us our false beliefs"[105]—which happen to include traditional Christian interpretation of biblical passages. For example, concerning the greatest commandment given by Jesus—to love God above all else (Matthew 22:38)—we are told it really means this: "Start with the first and greatest commandment, which is to love the Lord Self with every particle of feeling you have."[106]

What is most ironic is that the Scriptures are actually twisted by these so-called "angels" to deceive people into accepting their own demonization! Consider, for example, how three popular Scriptures are interpreted:

> If we are totally sincere and willing to surrender the lesser in exchange for the greater, the Holy Self will *gently ease the old personality out and will replace that lower energy with Itself....* An entirely new wine skin must be made ready for the new inpouring. Paul said, "I die daily" (1 Corinthians 15:31)—and this is what we must do to secure the final victory. Remember, "unless one is born anew, he cannot see the kingdom of God" (John 3:3). And "whoever loses his life for [the sake of the Christ within] will find it" (Matthew 16:25).[107]

In the end, to "accept Christ" is to accept the "angel" inside and to allow it to possess you.[108]

Most people assume that since these beings are allegedly angels, they would naturally quote Scripture—isn't this what we expect of angels? Further, "Could an angel possibly be associated with Satan?"[109] Of course not; who would ever expect such a thing?

Yet consider the following revelations from several popular angels and then look up the Scripture provided to prove to yourself that these beings could not possibly be holy angels: "You may think that there is only one truth; yet we, your angels, suggest that all of you have your own truth, your own interpretation of divine law. No one way is right or wrong"[110] (cf., John 14:6; 1 John 2:21); "[It is wrong] to feel that only one way is the authentic path to God"[111] (cf., John 10:1-12; Acts 4:12; 1 Timothy 2:5,6); "Love . . . is 'the capacity to allow all other living things to grow into their fullest expression of self,'"[112] (cf., 1 Corinthians 13:3-8); "In Truth I am the Spirit of God . . . for God is all, and all is God"[113] (cf., Ezekiel 28:2-4).

Now consider the following personal meditation provided by the popular angels, which they wish people to assimilate into their consciousness. Ask yourself if such statements could possibly come from godly angels: "All that God is, I AM. . . . I AM divine purity. . . . I AM perfect love. . . . I AM the peace that goes beyond understanding. . . . I AM omnipotent. . . . I AM perfect judgment. . . . I AM the only supply . . . the I AM THAT I AM . . . for I AM the joy of the world."[114]

19. Do popular angels appear in Near Death Experiences (NDEs)?

Near-death research also indicates the modern influence of "angels." Almost 15 million people have had what is called a "near death experience" (NDE). This is where clinically dead individuals have the perception of being out of the body, going through a tunnel, seeing a light, being enveloped by the light, and having some form of contact with a being of light, the dead, or angels. One of the most common elements is the appearance of a "being of light" (often interpreted as an angel) who guides the dying across the threshold of "death." In fact, many psychic nurses claim to see "angels" appearing to their patients at the moment of death to guide their spirits into the afterlife.[115]

Angels may be a frequent occurrence, or at least perception, in NDEs, but the messages they give are no different from those given in the spiritistic tradition in general. Unfortunately, the deep NDE is characteristically an initiation into the world of the occult, with far-reaching consequences. In *The Facts on life after Death*, we have supplied information evaluating the near-death experience and why we believe that the "being of light" or "angels" are not who they claim to be. We refer the reader to this booklet for more information.

20. Are popular angels related to UFOs?

Modern fascination with UFOs has grown by leaps and bounds since the first reported sighting by Kenneth Arnold in 1947. Today, the field known as ufology is a growing industry with scores of organizations around the world, at least a dozen government investigations, and literally millions of sightings—including thousands of alleged UFO entity contacts or abductions. Most people think that UFOs are either hoaxes, misinterpretations, hallucinations, or actual visits from extraterrestrial civilizations.

Probably the last conclusion is that UFOs are an angelic phenomenon, let alone a product of the power of fallen angels. But this is exactly what they are. Off and on for 20 years, coauthor John Weldon has researched this field and has written three books, including *The Facts on UFOs and Other Supernatural Phenomena* with John Ankerberg, in which he presents startling and convincing evidence that UFOs can *only* be explained by recourse to demonology.

21. What do the popular angels teach about ethics and the new morality?

Several books on angels actually tell us that Satan is the good guy! Given such a distorted sense of values, perhaps the resulting ethical views are not surprising. For example: "The Angel of Materiality and Temptation [i.e., "the Devil"] works with us.... It is the energy that enables us to say with understanding, 'I live, yet not I, but Christ liveth in me.'"[116] Another book on angels tells us that "Lucifer was really doing God's work."[117] Elsewhere, we are actually encouraged to welcome the Angel of Death!:

> To the average person the Angel of Death is most feared, but to the aspirants, disciples, and initiates he is "the one who is welcomed as the sunrise." Make contact now and ask him to assist you in preparing for the final step of release and acceptance.... Remember

there is no such thing as death, only a change of
energy.... In Truth that which we call death is but an
entrance into a more glorious life of joy, fulfillment,
peace, and freedom.[118]

The morality offered by the popular angels is consistent
with that found in the occult in general—a self-generated
morality achieved through "higher" consciousness that
allows one to justify everything and to live any way one
wishes. Those "angels" encourage this by endorsing such
things as free sex, homosexuality and lesbianism, adultery,
abortion, divorce, and virtually every moral lapse. Some
angels endorse these behaviors in the name of a "proper"
understanding of certain spiritual truths: that one must
move *beyond* good and evil to comprehend the underlying
unity of creation, or that God encompasses both good and
evil within His own being.[119]

Obviously, if the "higher" consciousness lies beyond the
categories of good and evil and if God Himself encompasses
both, it's going to be difficult to sort things out ethically. In
the end, selfishness, hedonism, and sensuality win the day:
"Morality ... involves making choices that are best for
you"[120] and "Most of all, the angels want to encourage you
to have fun, be wild ... The angels are attracted to free
spirits who aren't afraid of being themselves, even if the
bulk of society can't seem to understand them.... Our
imperfections makes us interesting.... It is okay to make
mistakes or to be 'wrong.'"[121]

We are also told to abandon our preexisting religious
beliefs and the rules that come with them because they are
far too restricting.[122] In fact, even deliberately practiced
evil is said to become a means to spiritual enlightenment.[123]

Do these statments sound just a bit too unorthodox to
really be the teachings of angels? Yet most people in our
country apparently believe that these really *are* the teachings of angels! But if so, then what of God?

22. What about popular angels, self-esteem, and self-love teachings?

Given the fact that the sin of the devil was pride and self-
aggrandizement, it might not be surprising that he would
find it difficult to relinquish the self-love that produced his
own notoriety. Unfortunately, people rarely comprehend
precisely where a self-love philosophy that mimics the devil's

own can lead them. Perhaps, then, those angel authors who are so fond of defining the devil as "ego-dominated personality" need to rethink the implications.[124]

In an age of the self, the modern angels fit right in.

One of the most popular teachings of the angels is that people must learn the importance of self-esteem and self-love:

> Self-love will nurture and nourish you....Forge ahead into the everlasting wonderful effects of true self-love....Simply allow feelings of love for yourself to emerge. Here they come. Now bask in the light of self-love....Eventually, you find yourself fully in the golden light as you step forward on the path of self-love with your angelic guide from the energy system of divine love. You thank your angel guide and then thank yourself....[125]

> You do not need to ask permission to love yourself...nothing less is sufficient to you or God.... [Claiming] your own goodness...[will] further goodness on the earth.[126]

The only problem is that all this self-esteem is based on the false concept that man in his true nature is divine; that is, "you are God," and "God is life."[127]

23. Do popular angels endorse divination?

Divination systems are as old as mankind and include such things as the ancient oracles through whom the spirits ("gods") spoke, the I Ching, Tarot cards, Runes, the Ouija board, and divination by everything from bird behavior and entrails to skull contours, palms, simple dots, and sticks.

Today, the popular angels have also entered the business of divination in a big way. In Alma Daniel, Timothy Wyllie, and Andrew Ramer's *Ask Your Angels* (1992), we find a five-step method called the GRACE Process. This divination method, termed the "Angel Oracle," is essentially a three-part deck of cards. The first cards are assigned to four archangels, and the random picking of a card connects you with the creative dreaming or problem-solving aspects of the specific angel on the card. The second set of cards has 16 angels, which when picked "activate" the angel associated with the card to help the person be successful in selecting from the third set of cards. This set has 24 activities or situations. Once one of these is chosen, the person is to pursue the card's instructions, knowing that the angel from the second set of cards will guide and direct him to the fulfillment.

Another system of divination is called Angel Cards. This includes a board game called "The Game of Transformation." It was created while the originators were living at the New Age Findhorn community. This game is also intended to establish contact with angels, predict the future, and to develop "higher" consciousness.[128]

A third system of divination is found in the book *Angelic Messengers Cards: A Divination System for Spiritual Discovery*, which was developed in association with the spirit guide "Mentor." This system uses cards with pictures of flowers, which one's angels then use to promote spiritual growth: "The cards act as a 'living prayer' to help us resolve problems, develop inner trust, affirm ourselves, and renew and awaken the spiritual energy of love.... The *angelic messenger cards* are a divinely-inspired tool for self-discovery and ... carry the seeds of both personal and planetary transformation."[129]

The problem with using any kind of divination method is that, in the words of occult authority W.B. Crow, it is "nearly always dangerous."[130] These systems are dangerous because, first, they link one to demons; second, the information derived is just as frequently *bad* advice; and third, divination brings a bondage to an occult system—it causes people to make decisions they otherwise would not.

24. Do popular angels endorse the Christian "faith"/ positive confession movements? How might popular angels indirectly infiltrate the church?

Many of these angel books seem to use terminology directed toward Christians. One particularly potent occult text encourages the reader to "endow each angel with the Will of God, the Love of Christ, and the Action of the Holy Spirit."[131] Author Sophy Burnham observes, "Why is it that angels like disguise? It seems they take whatever form the visited person is willing to accept."[132]

As we documented in *The Facts on the Faith Movement* and *The Facts on False Teachings in the Church*, the modern faith/positive confession leaders usually claim that they have received their unique teachings by direct divine revelation—including through the mediation of angels. In those booklets, we have proven that these teachings are not biblical and hence could not have come from God *or* the good angels.

If the claims of supernatural inspiration made by these teachers are legitimate, then only one source of revelation remains. Perhaps it is significant that many spirit guides today have an entire series of positive confession tapes which are sold by their mediums. (The tapes by "DaBen" and "Orin" include such titles as, "Creating Money: The Spiritual Law of Prosperity and Abundance" and "Awakening Your Prosperity Self."[133]

The popular angels also actively support and endorse positive confession teachings. As Terry Lynn Taylor remarks, "Angels are the missing link in the chain of... self-help, self-development, and self-reliance programs.... Angels are heaven-sent agents who are always available to help you create heaven in your life."[134]

The entire purpose of the book *Creating with the Angels: An Angel-Guided Journey into Creativity* is to use angels to create success in every area of life.[135] As one angel says, "Abundance is a state of mind that leads to physical manifestation of physical resources. But, more important, abundance is a state of spirit that initially awakens the mind to its creative possibilities. You are being led toward abundant thinking, feeling, loving, and participating in life so that you will be in a position to encourage wholism in every form wherever you find it."[136]

In fact, the angels speak in exactly the same terms and cite exactly the same Scriptures as some modern Christian prosperity teachers. In *The Angels Within Us* we read:

> The Bible also says, "By your words you will be justified, and by your words you will be condemned" (Matt. 12:37); "Death and life are in the power of the tongue" (Prov. 18:21); And "Thou shall also decree a thing, and it shall be established unto thee" (Job 22:28). Charles Fillmore, cofounder of Unity, wrote, "the spoken word carries vibrations through the universal ether."... And Ernest Holmes, founder of the Church of Religious Science has written, "The word gives form to the unformed."[137]

Or consider the following advice by the "angel" in this same occult book: "I have promised you unlimited prosperity.... I am the Lord your healer, I heal all your diseases, restore health to you, and heal your wounds. This is not to come. It is. In truth, you are healed now; you are whole."[138] Thus, the author tells his readers: "Make contact with the angel and ask how you are limiting your own success. Let him show you any false beliefs that may be blocking the flow from his perspective."[139]

Now consider teachings from other books on angels: "True abundance is the ability to see the abundance that is already ours."[140] "I harness the power that enables me to realize all of my desires and objectives.... I have the power to know what is best."[141] "If we believe that we can have something...our higher selves—the parts of our psyches that are in communication with the angels—will begin to create it for us."[142] "I create my own miracles."[143]

All this is proof positive that the modern Christian prosperity movement has aligned itself with the very *same* teachings given by the spirit world. Now, if we know that these kinds of teachings derive not from angels but from demons, and if we know that prosperity teachers claim to receive these teachings by supernatural inspiration, the conclusion would seem self-evident: Teachers who influence millions of Christians may perhaps become an avenue for the acceptance of demons masquerading as angels.

Consider the following and listen to the words of some of the faith teachers themselves before you make a decision.

Kenneth Copeland teaches, "When you use the Word in the name of Jesus [that is, in positive confession] they [angels] are obligated to follow your command."[144] Gloria Copeland suggests there may be at least 40,000 angels assigned to each believer, thus, "there is no shortage of angel power"[145] and "how long do you think it would take them to make you wealthy?"[146] Unfortunately, "for the most part, the heirs of the promise have not been using the angel power available to them."[147] Therefore, "Your words put the angels to work on your behalf to bring to pass whatever you say...the words of your mouth bind them or loose them to work for you."[148]

Charles Capps says God supernaturally revealed the same truths to him. In *Angels* he says, "You need the supernatural beings of God working for you here on earth."[149] In *Releasing the Ability of God*, he states, "The Spirit of God spoke this into my spirit just as plainly as if I heard it with my ears.... He said: *'The Word says the angels are ministering spirits. These ministering spirits stand beside you daily and listen to the words that you speak ... .but you are the one who tells them what to do.'*"[150] Therefore, "Angels will work for you. They will become involved in every area of your life—your home, your business, everything—but only to the extent that you allow them to operate."[151]

Prosperity teacher Kenneth Hagin claims that in 1958 "the Lord Jesus suddenly appeared" before him, with an angel standing three feet behind Him. In *I Believe in Visions*, he reveals, "He [Jesus] said, 'This is your angel.' 'My angel?' I asked. 'Yes, your angel, and if you will respond to him, he will appear to you as I will at times; and he will give you guidance and direction concerning the things of life.'"[152]

Jerry Savelle says that when we apply the principles of the faith movement "the angels come on the scene to see that what you say comes to pass."[153]

John Osteen teaches that "when you become a covenant-person, God assigns angels to watch you and your family."[154]

Robert Tilton says, "When you talk positively about your dream, you not only release its substance, but you release the angels to work for you, causing your dream to come to pass."[155]

Benny Hinn also accepts the supposed ministry of the "faith" angels.[156]

The concern in all this is that by teaching people that angels are anxiously standing by to do their personal bidding, these teachers are conditioning people to have a particular expectation about angels that is not biblical. To teach people that angels will give personal "guidance and direction" and that they "will become involved in every area of your life" and generate lots of money is exactly what channelers with spirit guides claim about the spirits *they* contact.

In 1987, Kenneth Copeland gave a prophecy "from Jesus Christ" in which "Jesus" promised that new and dramatic angel manifestations were going to increase in the church and that many "will have visitations from the spirit realm." Concerning the angels, "Jesus" allegedly told Copeland the following:

> A very outstanding time is on the way. A time is coming when there will be manifestation of angels more than usual, more than there has been in the past. Many of you are going to witness for yourselves the angel that has been put in charge and in command of your ministry and your life. Many of you are going to have visitations from the spirit realm.[157]

But this "Jesus" also denied his own deity: "Don't be disturbed when people accuse you of thinking you are

God.... They crucified me for claiming that I was God. But I didn't claim I was God; I just claimed I walked with Him and that He was in me. Hallelujah. That's what you are doing."[158] (See 2 Timothy 2:13.)

If Christians listen to such a "Jesus" and contact the "angels" he promises to send them, perhaps they should not be surprised at the outcome (see Ezekiel 13:1-9).

25. What about popular angels and other important methods of spiritual deception?

We think that the true reason demons are impersonating godly angels today is not only for purposes of spiritual deception, theologically and philosophically, but also so that the demons can more easily possess people in the guise of higher consciousness and "profound" angelic contact. To this, the angels must establish implicit trust with their human contacts. One way is by seeming to appear in a different nature and context than spirits that are traditionally deemed evil, or at least questionable, such as ghosts or poltergeists or seance spirits of the dead—allegedly confused, "earthbound" spirits. For example, *A Book of Angels* tells us that "when a spirit enters a room, you feel a chill... when it touches you or when its body passes through you, you feel an arctic cold.... *But angels are different, and no one who has seen an angel ever mistakes it for a ghost. Angels are remarkable for their warmth and light....* You are flooded with laughter, happiness.... Angels give aid, or bring messages of hope, but what they do *not* is wander, earth bound, like the lonely spirits who are dead."[159] (What proves this idea false is that there are many cases in modern channeling where the spirits act in the positive manner described, and yet we know these spirits are demons by the very messages they give.)

Another ruse is where the angels discredit the Christian interpretation beforehand. In this scenario, it is Christians who are agents of the "devil," pandering to false ideas and the consequences of their *misinterpretation* of angels as demons. As Rosemary Ellen Guiley emphasizes, "If we start mistrusting the agents of light, fearing that they are demons in disguise, then we paralyze ourselves—which is precisely what the dark side wants. They would like us to trust nothing and encase ourselves trembling in fear. Fear is the best weapon the darkness has. Fear is the fertile breeding ground for all evil.... The engines of darkness have terrible power, but nonetheless, they cannot stand up to the greater, more awesome power of light and love.[160]

Another deception is for the demons to be as kind, loving, protective, and humorous as possible in order to throw people off guard. "The angels love us always"; "I know that the angels are taking good care of my soul"; "Angels are truly everywhere—kind beings who only want to help and to love us"; "We, your angelic teachers . . . [promise] you are held eternally in divine love"; "We, your angelic teachers, ask you to accept that . . . your long-term best interest are always being considered."[161]

Such deceptions can only be true reflections of the demons' hatred for human beings.

Finally, consider the following teachings of the angels, which appeal to people's egos, to what they want to hear, and to their use of mystical intuition rather than rational thinking:

> Vulnerability isn't weakness; it is spiritual strength. . . . Living in the moment is one of the most significant universal teachings for improving the quality of your life. . . . Truth is the acceptance of your spirit's voice and a willingness . . . to honor the Force that brings you life. . . . Life is confusing when you listen only to your rational thinking. . . . We, your angelic teachers, expect nothing of you save that you listen to your heart.[162]

By appealing to human naiveté and the baser instincts in the guise of wonderful spiritual guidance, heaven, and enlightenment, demons are able to get people exactly where they want them. In our next question, we will see where this can lead.

26. Do the popular angels want to possess people?

For whatever reason, demons like to possess people. This is witnessed to by the fact that spirit possession is a universal phenomenon in pagan cultures throughout history. And with the modern revival of the New Age movement, the occult, Eastern religions, channeling, and now the popular angel phenomenon, possession is increasing in the culture of the West, which is itself being paganized in the process.

In *The Little Book of Angels* by Peter L. Wilson, we are told that not only can we worship angels but "there is another sort of angelic rite: one in which they are specifically evoked and called down, either to give and receive messages, or to enter into the body of the ritualist. In its simplest manifestation this results in the phenomenon of possession."[163]

Some angel books even assume that angels *already* exist within people, hence it is hardly surprising if advocates one day discover angels unexpectedly speaking *out* of them. *The Angels Within Us* is a book that teaches people how to become spirit-possessed under theme of spiritual enlightenment. It claims, "Within your individualized energy field, the microcosm called *you*, are twenty-two Causal Powers, or angels, that control your conscious behavior and govern the manifestation of all forms and experiences in your personal life."[164] At this point, possession is assumed whether or not anyone even believes in angels.

In some books, angelic meditations precondition the person to accept the concept of possession. For example, "I will unite my spirit with the angels" or, "We have the glorious opportunity to learn about the miraculous power of prayer and surrendering to a higher power."[165]

As in the world of the occult, various energy concepts are emphasized to rationalize possession by spirits as spiritual contact with the energy forces of Nature. Thus, one book uses the theme of Nature to mask a person's possession: "You are *merging* with those on *and off the Earth* who are *guiding your energy* because you accept a different future for humanity....So when you feel let down...talk to Nature. Nature is all around you no matter where on the Earth you live. Nature is all about *merger*, because it functions as one entirely interwoven system. You, like Nature, are becoming more and more *connected* with other light-workers in physical and *non-physical reality*."[166]

In other words, merger with Nature becomes the basis for spirit possession, rationalized as a merging or uniting with Nature's divine energies. In telling people that "love is energy,"[167] the message is given that possession by angels or their energy is a form of *love*: "Many cultures initiate their own spiritual students, and we, your angelic teachers, also initiate our own. Initiation requires you to release preconceived ideas about the period of training you are entering and to accept the higher good and spiritual guidance that places you under the protection and inspiration of the Universe."[168]

Consider the following statements by angels or angel authors concerning divine energies that can possess us: "Inner authority is spiritual energy born from union with the Divine."[169] "The spiritual energy of your life is welling up deep inside you from the core of your being and circling your spine to renew your life. You are in the process of managing this intense emerging energy so that you will direct it toward awakening the God within."[170] "Each time you allow this flow of creative energy—angel energy—to stream through your being, you expand this energy."[171] "The more that you are *aware* of this divine consciousness, the more its dynamic energies can fill the physical-plane person you thought you were. And when the infusion is complete, you awaken and understand that you embody all the Powers of God."[172] "It is the giving up of the personality, a replacing of the human consciousness with divine consciousness.... There is a fading out of one consciousness and a fading in of another."[173]

Consider the words of one person who "tapped into the energy" of an angel: "I felt a tremendous surge of energy move into my back and heard the words, 'I am the strength of Jehovah, mighty in battle to slay those who would defile.'"[174] In the same book we find the student encouraged to be possessed by the angel of death and rebirth: "This angel represents the force of metamorphosis, and its function is to... condition our consciousness for the final infusion of the God-self energy.... This divine agent [is]... the Master of Death."[175]

In most occult traditions the theme of death is synonymous with that of possession because the old person *does* die in the process of transformation/possession. In fact, they become a new entity in which their old consciousness is now "enlightened" and the possessing spirit has complete control— sometimes permanent, lifelong control—of the person's consciousness. This theme is touched on briefly in our *The Facts on Hinduism in America* and in more depth in Tal Brooke's *Riders of the Cosmic Circuit.*[176]

Of course, biblical or godly angels possess no one—there is no biblical record or historical account of a good angel possessing any person anywhere. Demons, of course, have a very long history of possessing people—and this is our final proof that the popular angels of today are really something other than what they claim.

Conclusion

We live in an age requiring a more critical attitude toward spiritual phenomena and religion in general. This includes many practices and beliefs that claim to be Christian. While no one can deny the vital and godly ministry of the good angels, no one should ever forget the multifaceted activities of the evil angels. To do so is to place one's soul at risk.

For those of you who have been contacting angels and yet now realize that they are demons, we suggest you pray the following prayer:

> Dear God, I now renounce my involvement with these spirits that I mistakenly thought were Your angels. I ask for Your protection from them. I confess my sin of seeking what You have forbidden. I believe that on the cross Jesus Christ died for my sin and rose again on the third day, and I now receive Jesus Christ as my Lord and Savior and ask Him to enter my life and make my life pleasing to Him. I recognize this is a solemn decision that You take very seriously.

Receiving Christ *is* a serious commitment. Please contact a local church where Jesus is honored or the Ankerberg ministry for helpful information on living the Christian life. ("The John Ankerberg Show," P.O. Box 8977, Chattanooga, TN 37414.)

Notes

1. In Marilynn Carlson Webber and William D. Webber, *A Rustle of Angels: Stories about Angels in Real-Life and Scripture* (Grand Rapids, MI: Zondervan, 1994), p. 19.
2. *Angels II: Beyond the Light*, NBC, October 30, 1994, host Stefanie Powers.
3. Ibid.
4. Cover story, *Time*, December 27, 1993, p. 58.
5. Cf., John Ankerberg and John Weldon, *The Facts on Islam* (Eugene, OR: Harvest House, 1992).
6. Billy Graham, *Angels: God's Secret Agents* (Dallas, TX: Word, 1975), p. 17.
7. Cf., M. Cameron Gray, ed., *Angels and Awakenings: Stories of the Miraculous by Great Modern Writers* (NY: Doubleday, 1994), pp. xv, xvi.
8. See John Ankerberg and John Weldon, *The Facts on Creation vs. Evolution* (Eugene, OR: Harvest House, 1993).
9. Timothy Jones, *Celebration of Angels* (Nashville: Nelson, 1994), p. xii.
10. *Time*, December 27, 1993, p. 56; David Briggs, "Heavenly Messengers Offer Comfort in Difficult Times," *Chattanooga New Free Press*, September 19, 1992, p. B5.
11. *Time*, December 27, 1993, p. 58.
12. Terry Lynn Taylor and Mary Beth Crain, *Angel Wisdom: 365 Meditations and Insights from the Heavens* (NY: HarperCollins, 1994), February 3, 23; May 18; November 16; and passim.
13. Cf., A.C. Gaebelein, *What the Bible Says about Angels* (Grand Rapids, MI: Baker, 1987), pp. 29-35.
14. Gaebelein, *What the Bible Says*, ch. 3; C. Fred Dickason, *Angels: Elect and Evil* (Chicago, IL: Moody Press, 1975), ch. 6; John Ankerberg and John Weldon, *The Facts on Jesus the Messiah* (Eugene, OR: Harvest House, 1993).
15. Jones, *Celebration*, pp. 3-16, 54-61.
16. Webber and Webber, *A Rustle*, p. 16.
17. Jones, *Celebration*, pp. 3-4.
18. Ibid., pp. 15-17.
19. Joan Wester Anderson, *Where Angels Walk* (NY: Valentine, 1992), pp. 26-27, 34, 46, 94-95, 121-124, 215-218, and passim.
20. Ibid., pp. 23-27.
21. Taylor and Crain, *Angel Wisdom*, Introduction and February 14.
22. Sanaya Roman and Duane Packer, *Opening to Channel: How to Connect with Your Guide*, (Tiburon, CA: H.J. Kramer, Inc., 1987), p. 43.
23. Meredith L. Young-Sowers, *Angelic Messenger Cards: A Divination System for Spiritual Discovery* (Walpole, NH: Stillpoint, 1993), pp. 209-210.
24. Terry Lynn Taylor, *Answers from the Angels* (Tiburon, CA: H.J. Kramer, 1993), p. 3.
25. Rosemary Ellen Guiley, *Angels of Mercy* (NY: Pocket Books, 1994), p. xv.
26. Webber and Webber, *A Rustle*, p. 180.
27. See Matthew 4:24; Mark 1:32,34; Luke 7:21; 9:1 and Kurt Koch, *Occult Bondage and Deliverance* (Grand Rapids, MI: Kregel, 1970).
28. Taylor and Crain, *Angel Wisdom*, January 4.
29. Ibid., February 6.
30. Ibid., October 7; Terry Lynn Taylor, *Messengers of Light: The Angels' Guide to Spiritual Growth* (Tiburon, CA: H.J. Kramer, 1990), p. 27.
31. Taylor, *Messengers of Light*, pp. 107-109.
32. Ibid., pp. 110-112.
33. Ibid., p. 111.
34. Young-Sowers, *Angelic Messenger Cards*, p. 58.
35. Ibid., p. 118.
36. Taylor and Crain, *Angel Wisdom*, March, 10.
37. E.g., Taylor, *Messengers of Light*, pp. 63, 139.
38. Ibid. p. 59; Taylor and Crain, *Angel Wisdom*, January 1; April 13.
39. Taylor and Crain, *Angel Wisdom*, January 1; April 12-13, 28; September 5.
40. See, "Brief Analysis of the Book of Mormon" and "Origin of the Book of Mormon" at the beginning of every *The Book of Mormon*.
41. Samuel M. Warren, comp. *A Compendium of the Theological Writings of Emanuel Swedenborg* (NY: Swedenborg Foundation, 1977), index references to angels, p. 749.
42. Cf., Rudolph Steiner, *Rudolph Steiner, an Autobiography* (Blauvelt, NY: Rudolph Steiner Publications, 1977); Rudolph Steiner, *From Jesus to Christ* (London: Rudolph Steiner Press, 1973); Rudolph Steiner, *Christianity and Occult Mysteries of Antiquity* (Blauvelt, NY: Steinerbooks, 1977), pp. 163-164, 168-172, and his lectures on necromancy.
43. Relayed to John Weldon from Jose Silva.
44. *Angels II: Beyond the Light*.
45. Charles and Francis Hunter (as told by Roland Buck), *Angels on Assignment* (Houston, TX: Hunter Books, 1979), pp. 22-24, 29, 52, 77, 81, 116-130, 142; James

Bjornstad, "Angels on Assignment" in *Institute of Contemporary Christianity Newsletter* (Box A, Oakland, NJ 07436), January/February 1980, pp. 2-3; "Angels on Assignment" by Leah Grossman and Walter Martin, Christian Research Institute Fact Sheet, 1979 (Box 500, San Juan Capistrano, CA 92693), pp. 1-2, 10-12.

46. J. Dover Wellman, et al., *The Christian Parapsychologist*, vol. 5, no. 7, pp. 220-221.

47. Ibid., p. 225.

48. Ibid., pp. 229-232.

49. Ibid., pp. 232-36.

50. Ibid., p. 240.

51. William Branham, *Footnotes on the Sands of Time: The Autobiography of William Marrian Branham* (Jeffersonville, IN: Spoken Word Publishers, 1976), p. 606.

52. Edward W. Oldring, *I Work with Angels* (Vancouver, B.C.: Note of Joy Books, 1979), pp. 14-15.

53. Ibid., pp. 126-27.

54. Ibid., pp. 65, 68.

55. G. Don Gilmore, *Angels, Angels Everywhere* (NY: Pilgrim Press, 1981), p. xi; cf., pp. 164-82.

56. Taylor and Crain, *Angel Wisdom*, Introduction and October 20.

57. See John Weldon and Zola Levitt, *Psychic Healing* (Dallas, TX: Zola Levitt Ministries, 1993).

58. Terry Lynn Taylor, *Creating with the Angels: An Angel-Guided Journey into Creativity* (Tiburon, CA: H.J. Kramer, 1993), pp. 153-154.

59. Gilmore, *Angels, Angels Everywhere*, p. 165.

60. Ibid., pp. 171-72.

61. Ibid, p. 173.

62. Ibid., pp. 173, 175-76.

63. Ibid., p. 182.

64. Ibid.

65. Taylor and Crain, *Angel Wisdom*, June 18, 28; July 8, 22; October 20.

66. Young-Sowers, *Angelic Messenger Cards*, p. 31.

67. Taylor, *Creating with the Angels*, pp. 39, 41.

68. John Randolph Price, *The Angels Within Us: A Spiritual Guide to the Twenty-two Angels that Govern Our Lives* (NY: Fawcett, 1993), p. 16.

69. *Angels II: Beyond the Light*.

70. Jeoffrey Hodson, *Clairvoyant Investigations* (Wheaton, IL: Theosophical, 1984), p. 2.

71. E.g., Don Fearheiley, *Angels Among Us* (NY: Avon, 1993), p. 94; Price, *Angels Within Us*, pp. 10-17, 32-33; Taylor, *Messengers of Light*, pp. 80-81, 111-112.

72. Taylor, *Messengers of Light*, p. 81.

73. Young-Sowers, *Angelic Messenger Cards*, pp. 14, 25; Phil Phillips, *Angels, Angels, Angels* (Landcaster, PA: Starburst, 1994), p. 122.

74. Karen Goldman, *The Angel Book* (NY: Simon & Schuster, 1992), p. 5; Karen Goldman, *Angel Voices* (NY: Simon & Schuster, 1993), p. 6.

75. *Angels II: Beyond the Light*.

76. Young-Sowers, *Angelic Messenger Cards*, p. 18.

77. Guiley, *Angels of Mercy*, pp. xi-xiv; cf., p. 90.

78. Ibid., pp. 97-98.

79. Ibid., p. 21.

80. Cf., Price, *The Angels Within Us*; Taylor and Crain, *Angel Wisdom*; and Guiley, *Angels of Mercy*.

81. *Angels II: Beyond the Light*.

82. Young-Sowers, *Angelic Messenger Cards*, p. 22, emphasis added.

83. Taylor and Crain, *Angel Wisdom*, December, 9.

84. In Guiley, *Angels of Mercy*, pp. 98-99.

85. Ibid., pp. 98-102.

86. Ibid., p. 105.

87. See John Ankerberg and John Weldon, *Protestants and Catholics: Do They Now Agree* (Eugene, OR: Harvest House, 1995).

88. Redemptionist Fathers, *Handbook for Today's Catholic* (Liguori, MO: Liguori Publications, 1978), p. 59.

89. Robert C. Broderick, ed., *The Catholic Encyclopedia* (NY: Nelson, 1987), p. 37.

90. Robert J. Fox, "Work of the Holy Angels Recognized by Church—Given New Norms," *Fatima Family Messenger*, October-December, 1992, p. 28.

91. Anderson, *Where Angels Walk*, p. 10.

92. Laeh Garfield and Jack Grant, *Companions in Spirit: A Guide to Working with Your Spirit Helpers* (Berkeley, CA: Celestial Arts), pp. 99-100.

93. Taylor and Crain, *Angel Wisdom*, August 15.

94. John Ankerberg and John Weldon, *Do Protestants and Catholics Now Agree*, (Chattanooga, TN: Ankerberg Theological Institute, 1994).

95. Sophy Burnham, *A Book of Angels: Reflections on Angels Past and Present and True Stories of How They Touch Our Lives* (NY: Valentine, 1990) p. 48; cf., Ibid., ch. 11.

96. Cf., Jay H. Lehr, ed., *Rational Readings on Environmental Concerns* (Van Nostrand Reinhold, 1992) and Michael S. Coffman, *Saviors of the Earth?* (Northfield, 1991).

97. Al Gore, *Earth in the Balance: Ecology and the Human Spirit* (Houghton Mifflin, 1992); cf., Berit Kjos *Under the Spell of Mother Earth* (Wheaton, IL: Victor, 1992) and "Al Gore's Environmental Spirituality," *The Discerner*, January-March, 1993.

98. Young-Sowers, *Angelic Messenger Cards*, p. 162.

99. Ibid., pp. 198, 206.

100. In Taylor and Crain, *Angel Wisdom*, April 30.

101. Ibid., April 20; cf., February 18, May 14, July 29, November 1, and December 8.

102. Cf., Paul Hawkin, *The Magic of Findhorn: An Eyewitness Account* (NY: Bantam, 1976).

103. Price, *The Angels Within Us*, pp. 60, 108, 114, 122-123.

104. Ibid., pp. 60, 122.

105. Ibid., p. 62.

106. Ibid., p. 63.

107. Ibid., pp. 189-191, emphasis added.

108. Ibid., pp. 187-91.

109. Ibid., p. 206.

110. Young-Sowers, *Angelic Messenger Cards*, p. 113.

111. Ibid., p. 135.

112. Ibid., p. 138.

113. Price, *The Angels Within Us*, p. 145.

114. Ibid., p. 276.

115. Cf., Joy Snell, *The Ministry of Angels* (NY: Citadel, 1959).

116. Price, *The Angels Within Us*, p. 215; cf., p. 212.

117. Guiley, *Angels of Mercy*, p. 221 citing English meduim and angel channeler Eddie Burks.

118. Price, *The Angels Within Us*, pp. 190-191, 185, cf., p. 212.

119. Young-Sowers, *Angelic Messenger Cards*, pp. 54, 82; cf., John Ankerberg and John Weldon, *The Facts on the New Age Movement* (Eugene, OR: Harvest House, 1988), p. 33, with *Emmanuel's Book III: What Is an Angel Doing Here?* (NY Bantam, 1993).

120. Taylor and Crain, *Angel Wisdom*, September 8.

121. Taylor, *Creating with the Angels*, pp. 4-6.

122. Taylor and Crain, *Angel Wisdom*, July 28; Taylor, *Creating with the Angels*, p. 37.

123. Guiley, *Angels of Mercy*, p. 222; cf., the Hindu and Buddhist traditions of Tantrism.

124. Price, *The Angels Within Us*, p. 165.

125. Taylor, *Creating with the Angels*, pp. 152, 156-161.

126. Young-Sowers, *Angelic Messenger Cards*, p. 98, 102.

127. Ibid., p. 118; cf., pp. 46, 54, 58.

128. Taylor, *Messengers of Light*, ch. 14.

129. Young-Sowers, *Angelic Messenger Cards*, pp. 24-25.

130. W.B. Crow, *A History of Magic, Witchcraft and Occultism* (North Hollywood, CA: Wilshire Books, 1968), p. 29.

131. Price, *The Angels Within Us*, p. 31

132. Burnham, *A Book of Angels*, p. 110.

133. Sanaya Roman and Duane Packer, *Opening to Channel: How to Connect with Your Guide* (Tiburon, CA: H.J. Kramer, Inc., 1987), pp. 231-232.

134. Taylor, *Messengers of Light*, p. xvi.

135. Taylor, *Creating with the Angels*, pp. vii-xi.

136. Young-Sowers, *Angelic Messenger Cards*, p. 214.

137. Price, *The Angels Within Us*, p. 268.

138. Ibid., pp. 263-264.

139. Ibid., p. 286.

140. Taylor and Crain, *Angel Wisdom*, February 8.

141. Ibid., January 11, 21.

142. Ibid., May 22.

143. Ibid., September 14.

144. Kenneth Copeland, *The Laws of Prosperity* (Ft. Worth, TX: Kenneth Copeland Publications, 1974), p. 104.

145. Gloria Copeland, *God's Will Is Prosperity* (Ft. Worth, TX: Kenneth Copeland Publications, 1978), pp. 84-85.

146. Ibid., p. 86.

147. Ibid., p. 65.

148. Ibid., p. 88.

149. Charles Capps, *Angels* (England, AZ: Charles Capps Publishers, 1984), p. 80.

150. Charles Capps, *Releasing the Ability of God* (England, AZ: Charles Capps Publishers, 1978), pp. 100-101, 105.

151. Capps, *Angels*, p. 173.

152. Kenneth Hagin, *I Believe in Visions* (Tulsa, OK: Kenneth Hagin Ministries, 1984), p. 93.

153. Jerry Savelle, *Energizing Your Faith* (Ft. Worth, TX: Jerry Savelle Ministries, 1983), p. 45.

154. John Osteen, *Unraveling the Mystery of the Blood Covenant* (Houston, TX: John Osteen Ministries, 1987), p. 45.

156. In *The Christian Sentinel*, vol. 1, no. 1., p. 13.
157. Kenneth Copeland, "Take Time to Pray," *Believer's Voice of Victory*, vol. 15, no. 2, February 1987, p. 9.
158. Ibid.
159. Burnham, *A Book of Angels*, pp. 17-18.
160. Guiley, *Angels of Mercy*, p. 217.
161. Respectively, Taylor and Crain, *Angel Wisdom*, November 6; Ibid., October 24; Ibid., November 16; Goldman, *The Angel Book*, p. 50; Young-Sowers, *Angelic Messenger Cards*, p. 146; Ibid., p. 218.
162. Young-Sowers, *Angelic Messenger Cards*, pp. 93, 105, 114, 121, 125, 146.
163. Peter L. Wison, *The Little Book of Angels* (Rockport, MA: Element, 1993), p. 50.
164. Price, *The Angels Within Us*, p. 9.
165. Taylor and Crain, *Angel Wisdom*, January 23; February 19.
166. Young-Sowers, *Angelic Messenger Cards*, p. 178, emphasis added.
167. Ibid., p. 213.
168. Ibid., p. 142.
169. Ibid., p. 97.
170. Ibid., p. 110.
171. Taylor, *Creating with the Angels*, p. xv.
172. Price, *The Angels Within Us*, p. 50.
173. Ibid., p. 187.
174. Ibid., p. 163.
175. Ibid., p. 183.
176. Brooke's book is available from SCP, P.O. Box 4308, Berkeley, CA 97404.